Wisdom from the Angel Oak

The Adventures of Brigid and John

Calhoun "Callie" Walpole

Cover art by Frank DeLoach

United Writers Press
Asheville, North Carolina
2024

ISBN: 978-1-961813-43-4

Published by St. John's Episcopal Church
in conjunction with
United Writers Press
Asheville, N.C.
www.uwpnew.com

Unless otherwise noted, photographs and artwork courtesy of:
Frank DeLoach: front cover, 14, 15
Jack Case: 12
Diane Dodd: 1 (2018 Sony's Pushing the Lense award-winning photo)
William Baldwin: 2, 8, 29, 30, 44
Anne-Clark Cromwell: 3, 6, 48
Bettie Tullis: 6
Grace Baker: 11, 19
Callie Walpole: 17, 22, 23
Gigi McShane: 21
Nancy Dutrow: 24, 25, 27, 38, 45, 47, 49, back cover
Zach Hyleman: 31
Rebecca Hyleman: 46

Most Sundays at St. John's Episcopal Church, in addition to a Sunday school summary led by extraordinary teachers Lucy and Thomas McAfee and the children present, we have a segment called "Lessons from the Angel Oak," in which the Angel Oak teaches young Brigid and John—and the children gathered—important lessons about life and faith, as well as love, hope, and hospitality.

ANGELED OAK

by William Baldwin

Acorn that squirrel squirreled away
may grow into a mighty oak—
If retrieved, though, and digested,
path leads on to lesser growth.
All a piece.
Way leads to way.
A buried acorn sprouts the oak,
and hence upon career, it'll
exercise such sovereignty
as purposeness subscribes
to all unfound, overlooked
mistook for dimple in the earth,
'fore giving birth to mighty tree.

ALL THE PEOPLE

Brigid and John walked to the Angel Oak and noticed people everywhere.

Brigid asked, "Angel Oak, do you ever get tired of all these people?"

The Angel Oak gave a graceful nod. "Of course, I get weary, but in the late afternoon and evening, I rest. There's nothing like a good night's rest to prepare one for the day to come. Besides, rest and welcome are the pilgrim way, and all these people who visit me are pilgrims—people on a journey. Pilgrims are to be welcomed."

"But all these people get in my way and sometimes they're loud," said John.

The Angel Oak smiled. "All are welcome here with me. All have always been welcome, and all will always be welcome. And you will do well to remember this in your own life. With me there's always plenty of room for others—especially those in need, just as there should be with you."

THE FEAST OF ST. MICHAEL AND ALL ANGELS

After church, Brigid and John ran to the Angel Oak to tell the tree that they had just learned about a special feast day on the church calendar called St. Michael and All Angels or, as it is also called, Michaelmas.

"Angel Oak, Angel Oak," said John, "It's the Feast of St. Michael and All Angels! Does that mean it's your feast day too? The front cover of our bulletin this morning had the word 'angel' on it!"

"That's a very good question, John," said the Oak. "You and I had not met yet, but Brigid and I talked about this the very first time she and I ever met."

"I remember!" said Brigid.

The tree continued. "What you see on the cover of your service bulletin is a marble plaque with the name Angel, which is located on the inside brick wall of the Angel family plot in your churchyard, that of St. John's Episcopal Church, where the Angel family were members. Brigid asked me how I could be both an angel and an oak. My name Angel comes from the name of that family. But the word angel, while lofty and grand—as you learned today—also means messenger, messenger of God."

At this point the Angel Oak's leaves began to flutter and the Spanish moss in her limbs began to sway. "Angels are all around us," said the tree.

THE BLESSING OF THE ANIMALS

"Angel Oak, are you coming to the blessing of the Animals this afternoon? It's at four o'clock," Brigid and John asked the tree in unison.

"Well, I'm sending my roots, and I'm sending my shoots. And I'll be there in spirit. I'm always there, just as I'm always here. I bless the animals every day, and they bless me. Like St. Francis, whose feast day you all are observing—there are some who think we were born around the same time—I bless the birds, especially the ones who find a home up high in my limbs. One of the things the mother birds like to teach the baby birds, when they are just learning to fly, is how to fly in a circle around me. As the babies are just learning, they feel safe staying close to me.

"Wow," exclaimed John, I'd sure like to see that sometime."

"So, Angel Oak," said Brigid. "You actually knew St. Francis?"

"Well," said the Angel Oak. "All creation is linked. You've been singing about it today. Several of the hymns you sang this morning—I could hear you all from here—are based on St. Francis, who believed the sun and moon should be praised, even the wind and rain and air and clouds and storms."

"What?" exclaimed Brigid. "Even a hurricane—how can that be?"

"Think about it," said the Angel Oak. "We who live on the coast tend to be careful in our prayers before a storm. We might pray for a storm to dissipate—that is, break up and cease to be a storm—or we might pray for it to go back to sea. But we don't pray for the storm to land south of us or north of us—because we certainly don't wish the storm on others.

As we prepare, we do all that we need to do, and we pray for safety for all. We are reminded at such times that we are linked to one another, and we pray for peace and calm—in the midst of all the storms of life. The storms of life will come—and some of them can even be defining moments for us—as we are given the opportunity grow, and even to reach out to others in love.

Brigid and John didn't know what to say. They had come to the Angel Oak for the sole purpose of inviting the tree to the Blessing of the Animals. Once again, the tree had much to share with them—things that raised more questions than answers.

They walked back to the church in silence—humbled to be a part of Creation itself. They didn't know it, but the ancient tree lifted her branches and blessed them on their way.

And St. Francis smiled.

SKINNED KNEES

"Angel Oak!" Brigid exclaimed, "Look at John's knee. He fell and scraped it."

The Angel Oak's leaves drooped ever so slightly. "I'm sorry to hear that, John. Let's take a look."

"It'll be all right," John said, showing the Angel Oak his knee that he had scraped while playing on the playground at school.

"Ah," the Angel Oak said, "I see your mother has put a nice salve on it."

"What is a salve?" Brigid asked.

"A salve, spelt S-A-L-V-E, is an ointment that is meant to soothe—to heal. To salve, or to make whole again," the Angel Oak responded. Then, as usual, the tree had a little more to say.

"Healing and wholeness are the business of us all," the tree said, as if speaking to no one at all and, yet everyone.

"I am only whole," the tree continued, "as I exist with others, drawing from this rich John's Island soil in which I am rooted and to which I also provide nourishment. But there are others who have worked hard over the years to protect me.

"For example, there was a very special opera this year at the Spoleto festival. The name of the opera is Omar. I could hear it all the way out here because the birds knew I would like it and they brought me the music. Toward the end, Omar sang,

'People of South Carolina, take care of the root of your tree.' Dear Brigid and John, that is the work. Care for others at their very core, at their very essence, trying to salve their wounds—as you allow others to care for you. That's what it's all about. Now run along, and I'll see you again soon.

FAITH ON EARTH

Brigid and John went to the Angel Oak to ask about "faith on earth."

The Angel Oak smiled. "Oh, yes, I know what you are asking about. Sometimes faith on earth seems difficult for humans—in part, because of how they treat one another at times. Humans can learn a great deal from me and other creatures of the natural world—God's own world—where we recognize that we are part of the circle of life."

The tree continued. "Look at me, for instance. Given my age and good health and experience in this part of God's creation here on John's Island, I have seen a lot. Some of it sad, much of it good. Faith on earth means co-existing and giving one another room to learn and grow. Faith on earth means putting one foot in front of the other and, in my case, sending forth my roots to other trees to support them and, among other things, providing oxygen.

"Faith on earth is an attitude—a way of living and moving and being. It means to have heart and not to *lose* heart—which is to say to be *courageous*. To have peace on earth, it is important to exercise not only love, but faith—it's about an action as much as anything.

"Dear Brigid and John, what does it mean for you in your life to have faith on earth?"

ALL SAINTS

"Angel Oak," said Brigid, 'Why do we always talk about the saints and why do we even have a special Sunday for them?"

"That's a good question, Brigid."

John piped up. "Yeah, I want to know too."

The tree explained. "I'm an oak tree. It could be said there's nothing really special about an oak. Oaks are not the oldest trees or the tallest; we are not the strongest; we don't produce the tastiest fruit or the prettiest flowers. But we oaks are adaptable. We are persevering. We can grow almost anywhere.

"In his book on oaks, William Bryant Logan wrote,

> 'Looking at an oak...we see not a world or a heaven but a unique living thing, out of a time even deeper than civilization.'"

The Angel Oak's branches swayed just a bit. "So, not earth *or* heaven—but both. Heaven and earth meet more often than we might recognize. Saints help us to remember. Some days we need to remember who we are so that we can become who we were created to be. The prophet Isaiah even urges God's people to be 'oaks of righteousness, a planting of the Lord,' to display God's glory. Another writer explains that 'God occasionally drops a handkerchief. These handkerchiefs are called saints.' Just as God occasionally drops acorns, which become oaks. I like to say to the baby acorns, 'Go and grow. Become who God created you to be.'"

The Angel Oak then spoke directly to Brigid and John: "I will be with you always." The children nodded. They pondered the tree's words and walked in silence back to the church, wondering how they themselves might grow.

SWEETGRASS

"Angel Oak," asked John, "Why isn't there any sweetgrass growing around you?"

"Well, John," replied the oak. "We are in a wooded area. Sweetgrass needs the sun.

"In times of old, the people who lived here would bring Sweetgrass and sit under my shade and weave baskets from Sweetgrass—what they called 'the hair of the earth.' Delicate—gentle, but strong. You see, live oaks are not the only plants on these islands that provide comfort as well as beauty and strength.

"May you draw from such beauty and strength."

CHRIST THE KING

Brigid and John were playing in the shade of the Angel Oak when John stopped and asked the tree, "Angel Oak, what is Christ the King Sunday and why were we celebrating it today at church?"

"Good question, John," replied the tree. "On your church calendar, you are moving into the season of Advent beginning next Sunday—you recognize Jesus as king as he is above and overall."

"Well," John asked, "Are *you* a king? Or queen? You're the biggest tree around."

The Angel Oak seemed to nod her branches. "Jesus taught us by word and the example of his life that to be great one must serve. It's not about greatness in the eyes of the world. Jesus turned the kingdom of this world upside-down. He showed us this when he took a towel and washed the feet of his disciples, and when he died for us on the cross."

The tree seemed to stand taller. "I might be one of the biggest, but that means I am the one who must serve the most—and give and nurture and love and welcome and build up. I could go on, but you and Brigid need to go on home now and finish your homework. You have school tomorrow."

WALKING IN THE DARKNESS

"Angel Oak," said Brigid, "we learned in church today that we are in the Advent season. We read something about how there were people who walked in darkness and something about seeing a great light."

"Ah, yes," said the Angel Oak. "People are sometimes afraid of the dark, but we need the dark. I need the darkness to rest properly. The days are getting shorter and shorter. We are reminded during this season that God is greater than anything we can imagine— yet he comes to us as a little baby—born in a manger among the animals. God loves us that much—to become one of us. Enjoy these few weeks before Christmas. Find time to rest and be restored as you prepare. Enjoy the quiet that the darkness of the night brings.

The Angel Oak's voice became soft and still, and her Spanish moss began to sway softly. Brigid and John walked back to the church in silence and wonder.

BRIGID AND JOHN MAKE A PATH

"Angel Oak," said Brigid, "look at the path that John and I made. Now we don't have to worry about getting caught by briars when we come to visit you."

"I see your fine path, Brigid and John," said the Angel Oak. "I am delighted that after all these years of our shared history you all at St. John's Episcopal Church have finally made a path to me, other than using the dirt road. We have always been connected. Have you ever considered why, on this vast island, the founders of your church chose to build so close to me?

"There's nothing like a path through the woods leading from one sacred site to another. Pathways connect us. Paths are like the roots of the live oak—my own roots, which travel far beneath the ground to find the roots of neighboring trees to link up, and share—to make a way, and welcome."

Once again, Brigid and John walked back to the church in solemn silence, holy silence. The tree blessed them on their way.

WHO ARE YOU? WHO AM I?

Brigid and John asked the Angel Oak why it isn't tall and straight like the pine tree. "Angel Oak, you seem bent over and your limbs even touch the ground. Why can't you be more like the pine tree? Then we could see you from far off. You would stand out above all the other trees."

"That is a very good question, children. But I can be only who I am meant to be," mused the tree. "Furthermore, I should only *try* to be who I am meant to be. To try to be anyone other than myself would be a disservice to the God who created me (and you). I began as an acorn. Acorns do not become pine trees. Acorns become oak trees.

"A wise man once said that each human being is born with a unique set of potentials that wish very deeply to be fulfilled—just as the acorn yearns to become the oak within it."

The Angel Oak paused. "Brigid and John, who are you? And how is God inviting the two of you—each in your own way—to grow?"

THE VIRGIN MARY, THE ANGEL OAK, AND THE DOVE

After church on the Fourth Sunday of Advent, Brigid and John went to see the Angel Oak. They saw what appeared to be a dove high up in the limbs of the tree.

"Angel Oak, is that a dove?" they asked. "We have a dove in our church, up high close to the ceiling."

"I know," said the Angel Oak. "The man who created that dove for you knew about the dove that lives with me—the Dove of the Holy Spirit. It's the same dove that approached the Virgin Mary, whom you honor today, Mary, the mother of Christ—the young woman who said 'Yes' to God."

Brigid and John were quiet.

"How about you, Brigid and John?" said the old oak. "Will you, like Mary, say 'Yes' to God?"

BABY JESUS WRITES TO THE ANGEL OAK FROM THE MANGER

To: The Angel Oak
Near St. John's Episcopal Church
John's Island, South Carolina

From: A Stable in Bethlehem

Dear Angel Oak,

The angels said they would be most delighted to deliver this message to you. They can get to John's Island faster than I can seeing as how I am a little baby. The angels are also a lot faster than the camels.

I have been meaning to write to you since long before I was even born. I am God, you know, which means you and I have known each other for a very long time, since before you were even a baby acorn. I just wanted to remind you that I am always with you, and I will always be with you. I also wanted to say thank you for being you—for continually fulfilling your purpose on earth—and over and under the earth—for loving and serving, which is all I really ask of anyone. Thank you for being shelter and strength for so many. Thank you for being mother and father to untold hundreds of thousands—and maybe more—and for offering shade and support for all who need rest and refreshment. Thank you for saying yes to my call to you to be an inspiration—and for always welcoming everyone with your broad arms. Finally, for now, thank you for the gentle lessons you regularly give to my two little special friends, saints in the making, Brigid and John. They love you, and I love you.

Jesus

THE STAR

Brigid and John asked the Angel Oak about the star they learned about in Sunday school and church—the star that led the wise men to Bethlehem.

"The star invites us to 'see and go' and 'go and tell,'" said the oak. "The star prompts us to move not only our feet and hands but our minds and hearts. The star even allows our proud hearts and stubborn wills to be put to flight—as our very soul tells out the glories of the Lord, the baby born in Bethlehem's stable.

"I'm talking about faith, dear Brigid and John. Faith is not only seeing and believing; faith is also about being and action. So go and tell and be and do. As you see the light—be light for others."

YOU ARE MUCH LOVED

Brigid and John were sitting at the trunk of the Angel Oak when they saw a dove perched on one of the trees higher branches. The Angel Oak said to them, "Brigid and John, always remember that you are beloved. You are much loved—and in you I am well pleased.

"These same words are the ones spoken by the Creator to his son, words the Creator speaks to us all—words to me and words to you. It is important for people to know that they are loved. And you two are much loved—by God, by your families, and by me, too."

"I love you too, Angel Oak," said John.

"Yeah," said Brigid. "Me too."

Brigid and John walked quietly back to church, pondering once again the deep meaning of their encounter with awe and wonder. The dove in the tree then flew away and up—higher and higher—as if to the heavens.

COME AND SEE

Brigid and John were walking around the trunk of the Angel Oak.

"Brigid," said the tree, "do you remember when you told your friend John about me? You described to him an ancient tree that could talk. You invited him to come and see for himself."

"I remember!" exclaimed John before Brigid could answer. "I was so surprised I couldn't even talk."

The tree chuckled so much that several loose branches fell to the ground. A bit of Spanish moss even landed on John's head. "The desire to share with others in such a way is a pure form of love," said the Angel Oak. "That's what the good news is all about—inviting others to 'come and see.'"

John heard the Angel Oak but he was too busy trying to remove the Spanish moss that had fallen on his head. Meanwhile, Brigid could not stop laughing.

And the Angel Oak laughed with them.

GOD GIVES THE GROWTH

Brigid and John were playing around the massive trunk of the Angel Oak. "Angel Oak, how did you get to be so big?" asked John.

"Ah, John," the tree replied in a happy tone, as always, delighted to have the chance to impart her wisdom to the young people. "One day, hundreds and hundreds of years ago, God dropped an acorn. That acorn sprouted into a tree and grew and grew. Over time, the Native Americans who lived here saw what was happening—they knew this soil to be sacred. And after all this time—here I am.

"You see, John, it's all about faith—and trust—that God the Creator will bring forth growth. Not only as God did with me—for you too. So, take heart. You are God's field—God's good and rich soil. What you do and who you are matter greatly. And remember, only you can be you."

Brigid and John skipped back to the church, happy and at peace, trusting both God and the Angel Oak.

UNITY, NOT UNIFORMITY

Brigid and John sat at the trunk of the wise tree, listening as it spoke of a man called Paul, who founded a church in Greece in the city of Corinth, a coastal city where many cultures and peoples converged.

"Paul loved these people," said the Angel Oak. "He wrote to them that he heard they were fighting with one another and trying to separate themselves from one another.

"Paul asked them, 'What on earth are you doing? Is this Lord, the Light of life, whom you now follow, divided? I think not. You can disagree all you wish but you need to remember that you are all one and you are to love one another.'"

The Angel Oak seemed to wrap its branches around the two friends. "That's what I mean when I say unity, not uniformity."

So simple, so hard.

SAINT BRIGID AND THE CHURCH OF THE OAK

When Brigid and John arrived to visit the Angel Oak, the tree was so happy it seemed to be clutching its branches in anticipation of the children's arrival. "What has taken y'all so long?" the tree exclaimed. "I am so happy to see you both!"

"What's the big deal, Angel Oak?" asked John.

"What's the big deal? Why this week is our own Brigid's special saint's day. February 1st is the feast day of Saint Brigid of Ireland. Brigid, you remember when we first met, you told me your parents named you for Brigid—who, along with Patrick is one of the patron saints of Ireland."

"Yes, I remember. But what's so special about her?"

"Well," the tree explained, "she was a very generous little girl. There are many wonderful stories about her. She liked to give away milk and butter to those in need and she often prayed. She founded a monastery and church under a large oak tree—one of my cousins in the Old World—called Church of the Oak."

"Wow!" John exclaimed to Brigid. "No wonder you like to visit the Angel Oak so much."

The tree lifted its branches as if in a broad grin.

Brigid looked up and smiled.

SALT AND LIGHT

Once again, the Angel Oak knew how to teach Brigid and John.

John asked the ancient tree, "Why are there so many trees like you in the Lowcountry?"

"You mean *live* oaks? Yes we're alike but remember that we are all unique, just as you, John, and you, Brigid, are unique. There is no one else on earth like you, and you have a special gift to offer to the world—which is yourself. You are to be light to others. But to answer your question..."

The Angel Oak always rambles so, thought John.

"We live oaks thrive near the coast and, while we don't do well when we're flooded, we don't mind a little salt spray. The salt makes our bark seem younger and more refreshed. Like you, we enjoy the salt air. And we do not mind sandy soil. In fact, we like it very much.

"So, go forth," continued the tree, "and be Salt and Light—a gift to be shared with others."

GET UP, AND DON'T BE AFRAID

The Angel Oak could see that Brigid and John seemed to be struggling a little on this particular day. The tree gently provided the space for them to talk and share.

John told the tree that he was afraid of not doing well in school and disappointing his parents. Brigid shared his fears. They both expressed worry about friends and how they felt left out at times.

The Angel Oak responded gently. "What you both have described is not easy but also part of what being human is all about. I want you to remember what Jesus said to Peter, James, and John when they heard the voice speaking from the cloud and then they fell to the ground because they were so afraid. Jesus touched them and said, 'Get up and do not be afraid.'"

"Besides," the tree continued, "what God spoke about Jesus, God also speaks to you—and so do I. 'This is my Son, the Beloved; with him I am well pleased.' You, dear Brigid and John, are also beloved—deeply loved by God—and me. So, get up, and do not be afraid."

YOUR SHADE AT YOUR RIGHT HAND

On this day the Angel Oak had a special message for Brigid and John:

"Remember, children, your help comes from the Lord, the maker of heaven and earth. The Lord will not let your foot be moved, and he who watches over you will not sleep. The Lord himself watches over you...

The Lord is your shade at your right hand, so that the sun shall not strike you by day, nor the moon by night.

The Lord shall preserve you from all evil...The Lord shall watch over your going out and your coming in, from this time forth for ever more.

Children, the Lord is your shade and so very much more. And so am I."

DEEP ROOTS, DEEP WELLS

Brigid and John learned about living water. The spring that year had been dusty and dry with a lot of pollen swirling through the air. The Resurrection Fern on the Angel Oak's limbs looked parched and lifeless.

John was curious and asked the tree, "Angel Oak, don't you ever get thirsty? Who brings you water to drink?"

It was as if the Angel Oak had been waiting for a thousand years for a little boy to ask it this question. "John, do you notice how my limbs grow very wide? Well, my roots in the ground grow very deep, as well as wide. They grow far enough to tap the water source way down deep in the very core of the earth.

"You see, my Creator knows what I need. And since my Creator is also your Creator, he knows what you need, too."

For once, Brigid was quiet. John seemed to wipe away a tear—a tear of thankfulness and wonder. That surprised him. He hadn't known that people cried good tears, too.

MUD MENDS

It was springtime and it had been raining for days. Brigid and John were a muddy mess by the time they reached the Angel Oak. The tree chuckled when then children arrived. "Well, you two certainly look like the John's Island children that you are—mud not only between your toes but on your face and in your hair!"

Brigid and John frowned.

"Don't be afraid of a little mud," said the Angel Oak. "Our Lowcountry plough mud is often used as a poultice—especially by those who practice the old ways. A poultice is a mixture that helps hurt muscles to heal.

"There's an old expression for when you want to wish someone well. When you want to wish them health and happiness, you can say: "Here's mud in your eye!"

"Here's mud in your eye to you, Angel Oak," John grumbled.

"Yeah," said Brigid, "I need to change clothes."

The children made their way back to the church and the ancient tree smiled.

I WILL PLACE YOU ON YOUR OWN SOIL

Brigid and John could not wait to tell the Angel Oak what they had learned in Sunday school about the prophet Ezekiel and his strange talk about dry bones coming back to life. They sang the funny song they had learned to the tree.

The Angel Oak was amused, as always, by the children. The tree said to them:

"The prophet Ezekiel goes on to talk about how God will place his very spirit within us—and we shall live. God also says: 'I will place you on your own soil.'"

The tree continued: "I grow the way that I do because I am where I am meant to be. The tourists often ask me how it is that I am so strong and healthy. I tell them that God has placed me in my own soil—just like Ezekiel says.

So, Brigid and John, remember that this rich fluvial soil of St. John's Parish is your own soil, too."

Brigid and John walked back to the church—beginning to recognize that what is below the ground—or below the surface—is sometimes more important than what is easily observed.

HEALING THROUGH WOUNDEDNESS

On the Second Sunday of Easter, Brigid and John ran to see the Angel Oak. They had missed the tree so much, what with the egg hunt on Easter Day and all the festivities.

John asked the tree a question he had been wondering about for a long time: "Angel Oak, why do you have a fence around you?"

The Angel Oak replied, "Well, John, many years ago sometimes people would come and paint or carve graffiti on my limbs, which hurt me very deeply. I still bear the effects of those carvings." The Angel Oak lifted up her limbs and showed the children her wounds. "Yet strangely perhaps, that began a process whereby my dignity and uniqueness began to be recognized and valued in a new way. It's not fun or easy, but remember, children, sometimes, by our very wounds we ourselves can help to bring healing—as Jesus did for us all."

St. John's parishioner Marianne Seabrook (now Stein) from a St. John's High School yearbook, 1960.

A VISION OF ANGELS

Once again, Brigid and John could not wait to tell the Angel Oak what they had seen. "Angel Oak!" they shouted, almost breathlessly, "We went on a visit to Wadmalaw the other day and we met a little live oak. Her name is Angelina. She started out as one of your acorns. She is so cute!"

The tree smiled. "Yes, I know. Angelina lives on Wadmalaw and is well cared for. The doves living in my branches often visit her and give me regular updates."

Baby Angel, who lives in a pot at the base of the Angel Oak, was waking up from his nap when he heard Brigid and John. "When can we go see her?" Baby Angel asked.

"Soon," the Angel Oak replied. "Soon and very soon."

TIME TOGETHER IN THE TEMPLE

On this particular day, the Angel Oak had a few things to say to Brigid and John. "Time together in the Temple," to quote one of your readings for today, "includes time together in church and time together here with me on these sacred grounds, which are God's. Worship is at the center of who we are and what we do. Time together in the temple includes this sacred place where untold numbers have gathered before you and will do so after you.

"You do not come to see me or attend church out of sheer obligation. You do it because it's who you are—and you never know how God might use the worship you offer. You do not rely on yourselves alone—you need the community that gathers with you. Besides, you never know how you might be transformed by your experience of worship—through your time together in the temple.

WAYS OF GENTLENESS AND PATHS OF PEACE

Brigid and John went to visit the Angel Oak the day after the coronation of King Charles III. "Angel Oak, did you watch the coronation yesterday?" asked Brigid. "We had to watch it because our priest said it was a liturgy. But there was a picture of you on one of the screens brought out during the anointing part of the service."

The Angel Oak smiled. "Yes, the Tree of Life. My ancestor. That beautiful image of the Tree of Life is a reminder that the One you follow is truly the Way, the Truth, and the Life. And that way is the way of love—the way of unity—paths of gentleness and peace."

Brigid and John and the Angel Oak heard a voice from up high in the branches.

"Hello!" trilled the Dove." "Did you see me?"

"I was there too."

"Of course you were," said the tree to the Dove:

"You are always there."

THE DOVE SPEAKS

Brigid and John returned the next Sunday to visit the Angel Oak. They were curious to see if the dove living high up in the branches of the Angel Oak would speak again. When they arrived at the trunk of the tree, they heard words they had heard that morning in church: "I will not leave you orphaned; I am coming to you." The children knew that it was the Lord, just as the disciples knew that it was the Lord when they were with him in the breaking of the bread.

At that moment the dove flew down to a lower branch. "I am the Spirit of truth you hear about. If you look closely over the altar at church, you will see me—the dove—the Spirit. I am with you always. In the words of Jesus, 'I will not leave you orphaned; I am coming to you.' Remember, children, you are never left alone; I am with you always; and I love you."

The dove flew up and up, higher and higher into the branches of the Angel Oak.

UP, UP, AND AWAY, BUT NOT GONE

Brigid and John asked the Angel Oak about the Dove. "Where did the dove go?

"The Dove flew up and up into a cloud. But the dove isn't gone. The dove will be back. What goes up will come down, but it may look different to you.

"In your psalm from this morning at church you heard the prayer thanking God for the rain: 'You sent a gracious rain, O God...you refreshed the land when it was weary.' God who is your Creator—and mine—always refreshes not only our beings but the very land itself. You remember that Jesus said that he will not leave you.

"Rest, children, in that knowledge and the truth of that promise. Pentecost is coming. It's next Sunday, in fact! Can't wait to talk then!"

WIND AND FIRE

"Good morning, children," the Angel Oak said to Brigid and John as they approached. "Don't you look nice in your red outfits! It must be Pentecost."

"Yes, it is!" Brigid exclaimed.

"You should see the hangings at church and the beautiful flowers," said John. "We learned all about the Spirit coming as wind and as tongues of fire."

"Yes," replied the tree. "I could see your tongues of fire a few weeks ago when you all finally burned that brush pile in the field out back. I was relieved there was no wind so that *I* didn't become a tongue of fire." The tree smiled.

"Remember, children, we all have our part to play. Even though we are different, the same Spirit who gives life to me gives new life and renewed life to you. So, trust the Spirit to do in you what needs doing."

GROUND, TRUNK, AND GREENERY

Brigid and John visited the Angel Oak on Trinity Sunday.

"God has been called the ground of being—the ground of all that is—above and below and upon and around the earth," said the tree. "We might refer to God's Son Jesus as the Trunk—the trunk of any tree, as well as me. Remember Jesus once said, 'I am the vine, you are the branches.'"

The tree continued. "Another word for Spirit is breath, so we might call the leaves, the Greenery and the Spirit "that which gives and reveals and indicates life." Ground, Trunk, and Greenery—and you, children, you are the branches."

Brigid and John walked back to the church, happy that Trinity Sunday comes around only once a year.

REST AND REFRESHMENT UNDER THE OAK

After hearing in the Book of Genesis about the Oak of Mamre—also known as Abraham's Oak—Brigid and John went to visit the Angel Oak.

"Angel Oak, did you personally know the Oak of Abraham that we learned about today in church?" asked John.

"Why, yes, I did, and I still do. Even now, after all this time, new life is growing from that ancient tree," answered the tree. "In the Genesis story, Abraham invites the three visitors to rest under the tree and offers them water and bread." The Angel Oak paused. "Children, I want you to see that gracious hospitality is what it's all about. Being open and welcoming to all is not only the way of trees like Abraham's Oak and me—it is also the way of God. Always remember to offer hospitality, rest, and refreshment to all."

BUILDING ALTARS

One pleasant Sunday morning in early June, Brigid and John listened intently in church to the reading from the Book of Genesis. When they walked down to visit the Angel Oak after church, they asked the Tree, "Why did Abraham build altars?"

The Angel Oak replied, "An altar is a holy place of meeting and gathering. It is a place of dedication and re-dedication of 'ourselves, our souls and bodies, to be a reasonable, holy, and living sacrifice to God.'

"An altar is a site of communion—of response," the Tree continued, "a response to God and to God's great love.To build an altar is to respond to the promise and truth and action of God in the world—for good—and for those who will come after you.

"So, go, children, go. 'Go to the altar of God, the God of your joy and gladness.'"

THE FEAST OF WILLIAM ALEXANDER GUERRY

Before Brigid and John could say a word, the Angel Oak greeted them. "Happy Bishop Guerry Day, children!"

"Wait..." John replied. "How did you know?"

"Well, Bishop Guerry would sometimes stop and visit me when he was on John's Island. He knew that I was always open to all, and I believe he even gained a bit of refreshment here with me.

From an icon of Bishop Guerry created by Christopher Rivers

"Some years after his death, his son Edward became the rector here. The bishop's calling was a high calling. But his calling is also *our* calling. The way of Christ is the way of the cross. It is the way of love. We are always growing— deeper and wider into the full stature of Christ. You, children, follow a martyred bishop and a crucified Saviour. That's your legacy—and that's the truth. And the truth, as Bishop Guerry preached—and lived—is for healing."

THE ANGEL OAK REMEMBERS THE REVOLUTION

After the marvelous Independence Day celebration at church, which was followed by hamburgers, hotdogs, and ice cream, Brigid and John walked down to see the tree. They began to tell the Angel Oak all about the day's festivities.

"Ah, yes," mused the Ancient Lady, "I well remember those days. I felt as if I were holding tight while the storms of skirmishes and battles raged all around me.

"I knew my role—always to be steady and strong and work toward healing when possible.

"Your church, the beautiful St. John's, which was built in 1734, lay in ruins after the Revolution. The roof was gone, the pews were missing, the structure was left entirely unsound. A couple of generations would pass before the church would be rebuilt."

"My work is also your work—healing, rebuilding, restoring, mending, loving."

Brigid and John walked back to the church, pensive but happy.

REST IN A SEA ISLAND RAIN FOREST

When Brigid and John reached the Angel Oak after church, they were wringing with perspiration from the hot, humid day. The rain the night before had cooled things off, but the still air had returned. It was summertime, ordinary time, in which the altar hangings and vestments are green, the color of life and growth.

Heat and humidity are part of it all and to be welcomed, relished, even, for they help things to grow, much like in a rain forest.

John ran up to the tree. "Angel Oak, you should have been in church with us today. They were singing your song! There was all this talk about the weary finding rest. It's so funny to me how you and Jesus always seem to say the same things."

The Angel Oak simply smiled and said a prayer. "I thank you, Lord, that you have revealed these things to children."

GOOD SOIL

After watering the new flower garden at church, Brigid and John made a hop, skip, and a jump to see the Angel Oak. "I want to thank you for your hard work," said the Ancient Lady. "Jesus talks about the importance of planting in good soil, but oftentimes you must work to restore and heal the soil. And I am delighted to see that's what you all are doing."

"Well, it's so much fun!" Brigid declared. "I like watering the new plants and watching the bees and butterflies enjoy the new plantings."

"I know," the Angel Oak replied, "I can see it from here. Young Mr. Cottontail has also been talking all about it. In fact, I hear he was just over there yesterday! Good soil is so important and even helps to absorb flooding during storms. But making sure the soil is good, children, is up to you."

THE FIELD IS THE WORLD

By the time Brigid and John reached the Angel Oak, the tree was already speaking to them.

"Today in church, you learned about the wheat and the weeds."

"That's right," John answered, "We're supposed to let them grow together."

"Yes," said the Angel Oak. "It's all about the support we provide to one another—caring and sharing and building one another up.

"The ecologist Douglas Tallamy, who is one of my good friends, has written the following line about oaks, of which I am but one:

'Oaks support more forms of life and more fascinating interactions than any other tree genus in North America.'

"This is my calling," said the Angel Oak. "To build up and around—and under the ground as well as above the ground. This, children, is also *your* calling—because, as Jesus said, the field is the world."

ACORNS AND MUSTARD SEEDS

John asked the Angel Oak if it had ever seen a mustard seed.

"Why, yes, John," answered the tree, "the mustard seed and I have a great deal in common. I started out as an acorn and look at me now! The mustard seed began as something even smaller, only to grow into something grand."

The tree mused for a moment. "I have noticed that humans sometimes have become so accustomed to wanting immediate results that it becomes easy to dismiss seeds and kernels and acorns. With time and patience and tender care, though, from small, seemingly insignificant beginnings something marvelous grows. We trust our Creator to do more than we can ever ask for or imagine—and good things happen in time—in God's time."

SHINING FACES, BEAUTIFUL PLACES

After a couple of days of steady rain, Brigid and John went to visit the Angel Oak, as they always did on Sunday mornings after church. The tree was startling in its green covering of Resurrection Fern.

John had been captivated by the morning's observance of the Feast of the Transfiguration. "Angel Oak," he asked, "have you been talking with God?"

The tree smiled. "Yes, John. The gentle rain of the last couple of days has refreshed the earth and all that is in the earth and of the earth, including me. Just as the faces of Moses and Jesus shone, so I shine with the sign of the cleansing, restoring power of God to renew and remake his creation. And that creation includes both you and me and all and everything around us. God is always talking to us and loving us. So, children, let your faces shine. Let your light shine."

ABOUT THE ANGEL OAK

The Angel Oak on John's Island, near the City of Charleston in the Lowcountry of South Carolina, is the icon of the Sea Islands and, arguably, the region. Icons do not seek to gather attention for themselves; rather they point us to something grander and deeper. Icons like the Angel Oak encourage us to look beyond, and above.

The sprawling, deeply rooted Angel Oak is named for the Angel family, who were members of St. John's and are buried in the churchyard.

The tree is reputed to be at least 400 years old, with some estimates placing her over 1,000 years of age. In a word, the Angel Oak, like life itself, is eternal. The tree has been a gathering place for all—from Native Americans of old who knew the tree to be sacred, to present- day pilgrims—numbering well over 400,000 every year.

The ancient lady has always opened her broad arms to all. In the words of civil rights pioneer Septima Clark, whom Martin Luther King called the Mother of the Movement, "Segregation was at its height, but the tree was not segregated."

ABOUT THE CHURCH

St. John's Episcopal Church, whose history is inextricably linked with her grand neighbor, the Angel Oak, is located on John's Island and serves the nearby sea islands, which include not only John's Island, but Wadmalaw Island and the islands of Kiawah and Seabrook.

The parish was established in 1734. The current church building is the fourth structure on the site. The first two structures were lost during the Revolutionary and Civil wars. The third building, built to be temporary, was replaced with the present edifice in 1955.

Like her neighbor the Angel Oak, St. John's is firmly rooted in rich sea island soil, but with eyes toward generations yet unborn. St. John's Episcopal Church endeavors to rebuild, revive, and renew, while serving as a place of peace, prayer, and hospitality for all who grace her grounds.

ANGEL OAKS

by William Baldwin

Her decision to live in the tree
Was not made lightly.
Her parents were quite upset
And rightly so. They wanted more
For their daughter (had hearts set
On her having a career that made room for
Husband, children and two pets)
But she chose to go unclothed
Among the highest branches
Of the county's oldest oak and so
Woke each morning to the cries of the paparazzi.
Yes, I've been to see this for myself.
Paid admission like the rest
And marveled at the sight of perfect pink flesh
Against a mat of gray bark, resurrection fern,
And those tiny fly orchids, Spanish moss, of course,
And two jet vapor trails cutting through
The blue beyond. Time seals all wounds
And sets the crooked hearts aright.
Peace to trees and the women living in them.

From Shade to Sun—from Darkness to Light

These live oaks were planted at the home of St. John's parishioners Lil and Porcher "Shay" Stoney on John's Island in 1995-96. They have grown from one-gallon pots sprouted from acorns from the Angel Oak.

Hope—always hope—does indeed spring eternal. Because our Lord lives, we too shall live. The Angel Oak, like life itself—and love—is eternal.

Photo by Shay Stoney

I am grateful to William Baldwin for his two delightful poems and extraordinary photographs, to Frank DeLoach (Art by Frank) for his marvelous paintings of the Angel Oak, to Grace Baker for her artwork, to cousin Rembert Herbert for his helpful counsel, and to Nancy Dutrow, Anne-Clark Cromwell, Rebecca Hyleman, Zach Hyleman, Jack Case, Bettie Tullis, Gigi McShane, and Billy for their lovely photos and gracious efforts in this publication.

I am thankful also for the people of St. John's and the Lowcountry Land Trust, especially Executive Director Ashley Demosthenes and Samantha Siegel, Director of the Angel Oak Preserve. Thank you to Vally Sharpe of United Writers Press for bringing this book into our hands. I am especially grateful to Nancy Dutrow for her exquisite design of this book.

And a special thanks to Senior Warden David Maybank, Bev and Wally Seinsheimer, Christopher Rivers, Benjamin Schaffer, Jane Spelce, Lucy and Thomas McAfee, and all the acolytes of St. John's.

Yours, Callie
John's Island, South Carolina
September 2023

Made in the USA
Monee, IL
29 October 2023

45003471R00036